BATTLE OF PLASSEY: A TURNING POINT IN INDIAN HISTORY

GOLU KUMAR

This book has been published with all efforts taken to make the material error-free after the consent of the author. However, the author and the publisher do not assume and hereby disclaim any liability to any party for any loss, damage, or disruption caused by errors or omissions, whether such errors or omissions result from negligence, accident, or any other cause.

While every effort has been made to avoid any mistake or omission, this publication is being sold on the condition and understanding that neither the author nor the publishers or printers would be liable in any manner to any person by reason of any mistake or omission in this publication or for any action taken or omitted to be taken or advice rendered or accepted on the basis of this work. For any defect in printing or binding the publishers will be liable only to replace the defective copy by another copy of this work then available.

Contents

CHAPTER ONE

Clive had been busy making the necessary preparations for his army's advance. At Chandranagar, a sizable component of it had been stationed. On June 12, he sent all the men he had to that location, along with 150 sailors the admiral had loaned him. Calcutta was then guarded by a few sick Europeans, some sipáhs to care for the French prisoners, and a few gunners to man the ramparts‘ cannons. On the 13th, he left Chandranagar, the Europeans traveling by water in 200 boats being towed against the current by locals, while the sipáhs marched along the right bank of the river on the high road constructed by the Mughal Government from Hgl to Patna.

Approximately 900 Europeans made up the majority of the force, along with 200 men of mixed native and Portuguese ancestry who served with the Europeans, a small group of Lascars, and 2100 Sipáhs. There were two light howitzers and eight six-pounders in the artillery.

[Note 1: See page 137 of Broome's History of the Bengal Army.]

{91}The day after the force had set out Clive despatched to the Súbahdár a communication tantamount to a declaration of war; and he proceeded, as he approached the enemy's camp, to act as though such a declaration had been accepted. On the 16th he reached Paltí, a town on the western bank of the Kásimbázár river about six miles above its junction with the Jalangí. Twelve miles higher up he came within striking distance of Katwá, the Governor who was supposed to be one of the conspirators. Clive, expecting that the opposition would not be serious, despatched to occupy it, on the 17th, 200 Europeans and 500 sipáhís, under Major Eyre Coote. But either the Governor had changed his mind or he had only feigned compliance, for he prepared to resist Coote's attack. Coote at once made preparations for an assault and took such dispositions, that the garrison, recognizing the futility of resistance, and fearing to be cut off, evacuated the place, leaving large supplies in the hands of the victors.

The next day, the 18th, a terrific storm raged, and the force halted. The day following, Clive, who had committed himself to the enterprise mainly on the conviction that Mír Jafar would support him, received a letter from that nobleman, informing him that he had feigned reconciliation with the Súbahdár and had taken an oath not to assist the English, but adding that 'the purport of his convention with them must be carried into execution.' This strange letter from the man upon whose co-operation he particularly {92}depended led Clive to doubt whether, after all, Mír Jafar might not betray him. Under this possibility, the sense of the extreme danger of the enterprise in which he was engaged revealed itself to him more clearly than it had ever presented itself before. To cross an unfordable river in the face of a vastly superior enemy, at a distance of 150 miles from all support, would, he felt, be a most hazardous undertaking. Should Mír Jafar be faithless to him, as he had appeared to be to his master, and should the English force be defeated, there would scarcely survive a man to tell the tale? Again would Calcutta be in jeopardy--this time probably beyond redemption? Under the influence of such thoughts, he resolved not to cross the river until he should receive from Mír Jafar more definite assurances.

The next day, the 20th, a messenger arrived from his agent, Mr. Watts, who was then at Kalná, carrying a letter to the effect that before he quitted Murshidábád he had been engaged in an interview with Mír Jafar and his son when there entered some emissaries of the Súbahdár; that, in the presence of these, Mír Jafar had denounced Mr. Watts as a spy, and had threatened to destroy the English if they should attempt to cross the Bhágírathí. This letter decided Clive. He resolved to summon a Council of War.

There came to that Council, about noon of the 21st of June, the following officers: Colonel Clive, Majors Kilpatrick and Grant, Captains Gaupp, {93}Rumbold, Fischer, Palmer, Le Beaume, Waggonner, Corneille, and Jennings, Captain-Lieutenants Parshaw and Molitor;--Major Eyre Coote, Captains Alexander Grant, Cudmore, Armstrong, Muir, Campbell, and Captain-Lieutenant Carstairs. The question submitted to them was: 'whether under existing circumstances, and without other assistance, it would be prudent to cross the river and come to action at once with the Nawáb, or whether they should fortify themselves at Katwá, and wait till the monsoon was over when the Maráthás or some other country power might be induced to join them.' Contrary to the custom, Clive spoke first, the others following according to seniority. Clive spoke and voted against immediate action. He was supported by the twelve officers whose names immediately follow his name in the list I have given and opposed by the owners of the seven last names, Major Eyre Coote speaking very emphatically in favor of action; the majority of the Council, we thus see, siding with Clive.

The subsequent career of Eyre Coote, especially in Southern India, proved very clearly that as a commander in the field he fell far short of Robert Clive, but on this occasion, he was the wiser of the two. Some years later Clive, giving his evidence before a Select Committee of the House of Commons, emphatically stated that had he abided by the decision of the Council it would have caused the ruin of the East India Company. As it was, he reconsidered his vote the moment the Council was over. It is said that he {94}sat down under a clump of trees and began to turn over in his mind the arguments on both sides. He was still sitting when a despatch from Mír Jafar[2] reached him, containing favorable assurances. Clive then resolved to fight. All doubt had disappeared from his mind. He was again firm, self-reliant, confident. Meeting Eyre Coote as he returned to his quarters, he simply informed him that he had changed his mind and intended to fight, and then proceeded to dictate in his tent the orders for the advance.

[Footnote 2: Vide Ives's _Voyage and Historical Narrative_, p. 150. Mr. Ives was surgeon of the _Kent_ during the expedition to Bengal, and was a great friend of Admiral Watson.]

At sunrise on the 22nd, the force commenced the passage of the river. By four o'clock it was safe on the other side. Here a letter was received from Mír Jafar, informing Clive of the contemplated movements of the Nawáb. Clive replied that he 'would march to Plassey without delay, and would the next morning advance six miles further to the village of Dáudpur, but if Mír Jafar did not join him there, he would make peace with the Nawáb.' Two hours later, about sunset, he commenced his march amid a storm of heavy rain which wetted the men to the skin. In all respects, indeed, the march was particularly trying, for the recent rains had inundated the country, and for eight hours the troops had to follow the line of the river, the water constantly reaching their waists. They reached Plassey, a distance of fifteen miles, at one o'clock on the morning of the 23rd of June, and lay {95}down to sleep in a mango grove, the sound of drums and other music in the camp of the Nawáb solacing rather than disturbing them. The Súbahdár had reached his headquarters twelve hours before them.

The mango-tope in which the English were resting was but a mile distant from the entrenched position occupied by Siráj-up-daulá's army. It was about 800 yards in length and 300 in breadth, the trees planted in regular rows. All round it was a bank of earth, forming a good breastwork. Beyond this was a ditch choked with weeds and brambles. The length of the grove was nearly diagonal to the river, the north-west angle being little more than 50 yards from the bank, whilst at the south-west corner, it was more than 200 yards distant. A little in advance, on the bank of the river, stood a hunting box belonging to the Nawáb, encompassed by a wall of masonry. In this, during the night, Clive placed 200 Europeans and 300 natives, with two field pieces. But in the morning he withdrew the greater part of them.[3] He had with him 950 European infantry and artillery, 200 passes, men of mixed race, armed and equipped as Europeans, 50 sailors with seven midshipmen attached, 2100 sipáhís, a detail of lascars, and the field-pieces already mentioned.

[Footnote 3: Vide Orme's _History of India_, and Broome's _History of the Bengal Army_.]

On the spot which the Nawáb had selected for his entrenched camp, the river makes a bend in the form of a horseshoe, with the points much contracted, {96}forming a peninsula of about three miles in circumference, the neck of which was less than a quarter of a mile in breadth. The entrenchment commenced a little below the southern point of this gorge, resting on the river, extending inland for about 200 yards, and sweeping thence round to the north for about three miles. At this angle was a redoubt, on which the enemy had mounted several pieces of cannon. About 300 yards to the eastward of this redoubt was a hillock covered with jungle, and about 800 yards to the south, nearer Clive's grove, was a tank, and 100 yards further south was a second and larger one. Both of these were surrounded by large mounds of earth, and, with the hillock, formed important positions for either army to occupy. Thc Súbahdár's army was encamped partly in this peninsula, partly in the rear of the entrenchment. He had 50,000 infantry of sorts, 18,000 horses of better quality, and 53 guns, mostly 32, 24, and 18-pounders. The infantry was armed chiefly with matchlocks, swords, pikes, bows, and arrows, and possessed little or no discipline; the cavalry was well-trained and well-mounted; the guns were mounted on large platforms, furnished with wheels, and drawn by forty or fifty yokes of powerful oxen, assisted by elephants. But the most efficient portion of his force was a small party of forty to fifty Frenchmen, commanded by M. St. Frais, formerly one of the Council of Chandranagar. This party had attached to it four light field pieces.[4]

[Footnote 4: For these details see Orme, Broome, Clive's _Evidence before the Committee of the House of Commons_, Clive's _Report to the Court of Directors_, Sir Eyre Coote's _Narrative_, and Ives's _Voyage and Historical Narrative_. The account which follows is based entirely on these authorities.]

{97}At daybreak on the 23rd of June the Nawáb moved his entire army out of the entrenchment and advanced towards the position occupied by Clive, the several corps marching in compact order. In front was St. Frais, who took post at the larger tank, that nearest Clive's grove. On a line to his right, near the river, were a couple of heavy guns, under the orders of a native officer. Behind these two advanced parties, and within supporting distance, was a chosen body of 5000 horses and 7000 feet, under the immediate command of the Nawáb's most faithful general, Mír Madan.[5] The rest of the Nawáb's army extended in a curve, its right resting on the hillock near the camp; thence sweeping round in dense columns of horse and foot to the eastward of the southeast angle of the grove. Here, nearest to the English were placed the troops of Mír Jafar, then those of Yár Lutf Khán, beyond these Rájá Duláb Rám. The English within the grove was thus almost surrounded by the river and the enemy; but given the promised treachery of Mír Jafar, the greatest danger was to be apprehended from their immediate front, viz. from St. Frais, with his little body of Frenchmen, and from Mír Madan.

[Footnote 5: See Elliot's _History of India_, vol. viii. p. 428.]

From the roof of the hunting house, Clive watched his enemy take up the positions which would hold {98}him, if their generals were true to their master, in a vice. 'They approached apace,' he wrote in a letter of July 26 to the Secret Committee of the Court of Directors, 'and by six began to attack us with several heavy cannon, supported by the whole army, and continued to play on us very briskly for several hours, during which our situation was of the utmost service to us, being lodged in a large grove, with good mud banks. To succeed in an attempt on their cannon was next to impossible, as they were planted in a manner round us, and at considerable distances from each other. We, therefore, remained quiet in our post, in expectation of a successful attack upon their camp at night. About noon the enemy drew off their artillery and returned to their camp.'

So far, up to mid-day, we have the outline of the fight as narrated by Clive; it is, however, but an outline. It would seem that the action commenced by a discharge of one of the four guns of St. Frais. This discharge killed one and wounded another of the men of the European battalion. Immediately afterward the whole of the enemy's guns opened fire, but their shots flew high and did but little mischief. Clive meanwhile had drawn up his troops in line in front of the grove, their left resting on the hunting box, except two guns and two howitzers which he had posted at some brick kilns some 200 yards in front of the hunting box spoken of. These, as soon as the enemy opened, replied promptly and effectively. The remaining six guns, placed three on {99}each flank of the European battalion which formed the center of his line, answered the heavy batteries of the enemy, but, from their small caliber, made but little impression.

After a cannonade of half an hour, the English having lost ten Europeans and twenty sipáhís in killed and wounded, Clive withdrew them under the shelter of the grove, leaving one detachment at the brick kilns, another at the hunting box. This retrograde movement greatly encouraged the enemy. They brought their guns much nearer, and their fire became more vigorous and sustained. But its effect was less fatal, for the English troops were protected by the trees and the mud bank, and, sitting down, were but little exposed. This warfare continued till about eleven o'clock, the casualties being far greater on the side of the Nawáb's army than among the English. Then Clive summoned his principal officers to a conference, and it was resolved that the troops should occupy their existing positions until midnight, and should then attack the Nawáb's camp. We may regard the close of the conference as occurring about the same time as the withdrawal of the enemy's artillery indicated by Clive in the above extract from his despatch.

For, scarcely was the conference over, then the skies poured down a fierce shower, such as occurs often during the rainy season, which lasted an hour. Then it was that the enemy's artillery fire slackened by degrees almost to the point of ceasing, for the rain had damaged their ammunition, left almost completely {100}without cover. Clive had been more careful of his powder, so that when the enemy's horse, believing the English guns as powerless as their own, advanced towards the grove to charge, they were received with a fire that emptied many a saddle, and sent them reeling back. In this charge, Mír Madan, previously referred to, was killed.[6]

[Footnote 6: Elliot states, on the authority of the J'ami'ut Taw'ari'kh, that he was accidentally struck by a cannonball. _History of India_,.]

The death of this brave and faithful soldier greatly disheartened the Súbahdár. He sent for Mír Jafar and implored him to remain faithful to his oath. Taking off his turban and casting it at the feet of his uncle,[7] he exclaimed in humble tones, 'Jafar, that turban thou must defend.' Mír Jafar promised, but instead of performing, the degenerate Muhammadan returned to his confederates and sent a despatch to Clive, informing him of all that had passed, and begging him to push on immediately, or, if that were impossible, not to fail to attack during the night. His letter did not reach Clive till late in the evening. Meanwhile, other influences had been at work to bring about a similar result.

[Footnote 7: Mír Jafar had married the sister of Alí Vardi Khán, the Nawáb's father.]

It is impossible not to feel sympathy for the youthful prince, surrounded by traitors, his one true adherent killed. Scarcely had Mír Jafar quitted him when there came to him another traitor, Rájá Duláb Rám, who commanded the army corps nearest to the position {101}he had taken. The Rájá found his master in a state of great agitation. The English were showing themselves in the open; his men were giving way; hope was vanishing quickly. Instead of encouraging the Súbahdár to fight it out, the treacherous Rájá gave fuel to his fears, told him the day was lost and urged him to flee to Murshidábád. In an evil hour for his dynasty and himself, Siráj-up-daulá yielded to his persuasions, and, ordering his troops to retire within the intrenchment, mounted a swift dromedary, and fled, accompanied by 2000 horsemen, to his capital.

It was then two o'clock. The first hour since Clive's conference had been marked by the heavy rain; the second by the repulse of the Súbahdár's horsemen; the following up of the repulsed attack; the conversations of the Súbahdár with his two treacherous generals. By two o'clock the enemy's attack had completely ceased, and they were observed yoking their oxen preparatory to withdrawing within the entrenchment as the Súbahdár had ordered. There remained only on the ground that body of forty gallant Frenchmen under St. Frais, whom I have described as occupying the ground about the larger tank, that nearest to the grove. The post was an important one, for from it the English could have taken the retreating enemy in flank, and have inflicted heavy loss upon them. St. Frais was nearly isolated, but he, too, had seen the advantage the English would derive from occupying the position, and, faithful amid the faithless, he, with the gallantry of his nation, {102}resolved to defend it until it should be no longer defensible.

There was with the army a very gallant officer, Major James Kilpatrick, who had greatly distinguished himself in Southern India, and who, on this occasion, commanded the Company's troops. Kilpatrick had noted the firm front displayed by St. Frais, the great advantage to be derived from occupying the position he held, and the disadvantage of leaving him to hold it whilst the English force should advance. He resolved, then, to expel him: so sending word to Clive of his intentions, and of the reason which prompted his action, he marched with two companies towards St. Frais.

Clive, meanwhile, seeing the enemy's attack broken, yet deeming it better, not having received Mír Jafar's letter, to wait till the sun should have descended before making the decisive attack, had proceeded to the hunting box to rest after so many hours of fatigue and excitement, to be followed, he believed, by many more, having first given orders that he should be informed of any change that might occur in the enemy's position. He was there when the message of Kilpatrick reached him. Rising, he hurried to the spot, met Kilpatrick as he was advancing to the assault, reprimanded him for having taken such a step without orders, but seeing him so far forward, he took himself the command of the detachment, sending back Kilpatrick to the grove to bring the remainder of the troops. When St. Frais recognized {103}the earnestness of the English, and that he was entirely without support, he evacuated the post and retreated to the redoubt at the corner of the entrenchment. There he placed his guns ready for action.[8]

[Footnote 8: This episode is not specially mentioned by Clive, but it rests on irrefragable evidence. Vide Orme, vol. ii. p. 176: see also Sir Eyre Coote's _Narrative_; also Malcolm's _Life of Lord Clive_, vol. i. p. 260.]

Meanwhile, whilst the English force was thus advancing, the army corps commanded by Mír Jafar was observed to linger behind the rest of the retreating enemy. It was noticed, further, that when it had advanced almost abreast of the northern line of the grove, it faced to its left and advanced in that direction. For a time it seemed to the English officers as though the troops composing it were about to make a raid on their baggage, and a party with a field piece was sent forward to check them. The corps then halted, remained so for a time, then slowly retired, taking, however, a direction which led it apart from the other corps of the enemy. We shall return to them in a few moments.

Whilst this corps was executing the maneuver I have described, Clive had advanced to a position whence he could cannonade the enemy's camp. The effect of this fire was to cause great loss and confusion amongst the troops of the Súbahdár, at the same time that the English, giving, by their advance, their flank to the French in the redoubt, suffered also. To put {104}an end to this cross-fire Clive saw that the one remedy was to storm the redoubt. He was unwilling, however, to risk his troops in a severe contest with the French so long as the army corps, the movements of which I have described in the preceding paragraph should continue to occupy its threatening position. That corps might be the corps of Mír Jafar, but there was no certainty that it was so, for Clive had not then received Mír Jafar's letter, nor was he aware of the flight of the Nawáb. It was just at this critical moment that he observed the corps in question making the retrograde movement I have referred to. Then all doubt was over in his mind. It must, he was convinced, be the corps of his adherent. Certain now that he would not be molested, he hurled his troops against the redoubt and the hillock to the east of it. St. Frais displayed a bold front, but, abandoned almost immediately by his native allies, and deeming it wiser to preserve his handful of Europeans for another occasion, he evacuated the redoubt, leaving his field pieces behind him. His resistance was the last opposition offered to the English. The clocks struck five as he fell back, thus tolling the memorable hour which gave to England the richest province in India; which imposed upon her the necessity to advance upwards from its basis until she should reach the rocky region called with some show of reason the 'Glacis of the Fortress of Hindustán.'

Just as the beaten and the betrayed army was moving {105}off with its impedimenta, its elephants, its camels, leaving to be scrambled for an enormous mass of baggage, stores, cattle, and camp equipage, Clive received messengers from Mír Jafar requesting an interview. Clive replied by appointing a meeting for the morrow at Dáudpur, a village twenty miles to the south of Murshidábád. Thither the bulk of the troops, their spirits cheered by the promise made them that they would receive a liberal donation in money, marched that evening; whilst a detachment under Eyre Coote went forward in pursuit, to prevent the enemy from rallying. After a short halt, to enable the commissariat to exchange their small and worn-out bullocks for the splendid oxen of the Súbahdár, the troops pressed on, and at eight o'clock the entire force was united at Dáudpur.

Such was the battle of Plassey. The loss of the English force was extremely small, amounting to seven Europeans and sixteen sipáhís killed, and thirteen Europeans and thirty-six sipáhís wounded. No officer was killed: two were wounded, but their names are not recorded. A midshipman of the _Kent_, Shoreditch by name, was shot in the thigh, whilst doing duty with the artillery. The enemy's casualties were far greater. It was calculated to be, in killed and wounded, about a thousand, including many officers. They had been far more exposed than the English. Writing, in the letter already referred to, of the phases of the action between two and five o'clock, Clive states that their horse exposed {106}themselves a great deal; that 'many of them were killed, amongst the rest four or five officers of the first distinction.'

Clive had achieved success. Now, we need to document how he used it.

Chapter X: Clive's dealings with Mr. Jafar, the princes of Southern India, and the Dutch on the spoils of Plassey

Mr. Scrafton and Omar Beg[1] were sent by Clive the following morning to accompany Mr. Jafar to his camp. The time had come to divide at least one of the Plassey's treasures.

Omar Beg was Mr. Jafar's private agent who was assigned to Clive's person [Footnote 1:

Long previous to the battle Clive had received various proposals from the three general officers who had commanded the three principal army corps at Plassey. First, Yár Lutf Khán had made him a bid, his main condition being that he should be proclaimed Súbahdár.[2] Then Mír Jafar outbid him, bringing with him Rájá Duláb Rám, who would be content with the office of Finance Minister under the Mír. It had been arranged that whilst Mír Jafar should be proclaimed Súbahdár of the three provinces, he should confirm to the English all the advantages ceded by Siráj-up-daulá in the preceding February; should grant to the Company all the lands lying to the south of Calcutta, together with a slip of ground, {108}600 yards wide, all round the outside of the Maráthá Ditch;[3] should cede all the French factories and establishments in the province; should pledge himself that neither he nor his successors in the office of Súbahdár should erect fortifications below the town of Húglí; whilst he and they should give to, and require from, the English, support in case of hostilities from any quarter. Mír Jafar covenanted likewise to make very large payments to the Company and others under the name of restitution for the damages they had suffered since the first attack on Calcutta; others also under the title of gratification for services to be rendered in placing him on the _masnad_.[4] In the former category were reckoned one karor, or ten million, of rupees to be paid to the Company; ten lakhs to the native inhabitants of Calcutta, and seven lakhs to the Armenians. Undcr the second head payments were to be made to the army, the squadron, and the members of the Special Committee of Calcutta, to the extent noted below.[5]

[Footnote 2: The Nawáb, or Sbahdár, as he is more often known, was the formal title of the Bengali governor.]

[Footnote 3: It should be remembered that the Maráthás were regarded as significant and formidable adversaries in those days. The "Maratha Ditch" that encircles Calcutta was constructed in opposition to their ravages.

[Footnote 4: Masnad, a cushion, represents the seat of absolute power.]

[Footnote 5: The Squadron was to receive 2,500,000 rupees; the Army, the same; Mr. Drake, Governor of Calcutta (the same who had quitted Calcutta and his companions to take shelter on board ship at the time of Siráj-up-daulá's attack), 280,000; Colonel Clive, as second in the Select Committee (appointed before the war to negotiate with Mír Jafar), 280,000; Major Kilpatrick, Mr. Watts, and Mr. Becher, as members of the said Committee, 240,000 each. I may here state in anticipation that, in addition to these sums, the following private donations were subsequently given, viz.: to Clive, 1,600,000 rupees; to Watts, 300,000; to the six members of Council, 100,000 each; to Walsh, Clive's secretary and paymaster to the Madras troops, 500,000; to Scrafton, 200,000; to Lushington, 50,000; to Major A. Grant, commanding the detachment of H.M.'s 39th regiment, 100,000.]

{109}The first of these contracts, now become binding, was to be carried out on the morning of the 24th of June, at the interview between the two principal parties, Clive and Mír Jafar. It has occurred to me that the reader may care to know something more, little though it is, of the antecedents of this general, who, to his subsequent unhappiness, betrayed his master for his gain.

Mír Muhammad Jafar was a nobleman whose family had settled in Bihár. He had taken service under, had become a trusted officer of, Alí Vardi Khán, the father of Siráj-up-daulá, and had married his sister. On his death, he had been made Bakhshí, or Commander-in-chief, of the army, and, in that capacity, had commanded it when it took Calcutta in June 1756.[6] Between himself and his wife's nephew, Siráj-up-daulá, there had never been any cordiality. The latter, with the insolence of untamed and uneducated youth, had kicked against the authority of his uncle; had frequently insulted him; and had even removed him from his office. Mír Jafar had felt these slights bitterly. {110}Living, as he was, in an age of revolution, dynasties falling about him, the very throne of Delhi the appanage of the strongest, he felt no compunction in allying himself with the foreigner to remove from the throne--for it was virtually a throne--of Murshidábád the man who alternately insulted and fawned upon him. Little did he know, little even did he reck, the price he would have to pay. Fortunately for his peace of mind at the moment, the future was mercifully hidden from him. But those who are familiar with the history of Bengal after the first departure thence of Clive for England will admit that never did treason so surely find its punishment as did the treason of Mír Jafar.

[Footnote 6: There can be no doubt about this. 'About five o'clock the Nawáb entered the fort, carried in an open litter, attended by Mír Jafar Khán, his Bakhshí or General-in-chief, and the rest of his principal officers.' He was present when the English were brought before the Nawáb: vide Broome, p. 66. Orme, vol. ii. p. 73, makes a similar statement.]

But he is approaching now, with doubt and anxiety as to his reception, the camp in which he is to receive from his confederate the reward of treason, or reproaches for his want of efficient co-operation on the day preceding. On reaching the camp, writes the contemporaneous historian of the period,[7] 'he alighted from his elephant, and the guard drew out and rested their arms, to receive him with the highest honors. Not knowing the meaning of this compliment, he drew back, as if he thought it preparation for his destruction; but Colonel Clive, advancing hastily, embraced him, and saluted him Súbahdár of Bengal, Bihár, and Orissa, which removed his fears.' They discoursed then for about an hour. Clive pressed upon him the great necessity of proceeding at once to {111}Murshidábád to look after Siráj-up-daulá and to prevent the plunder of the treasury. The new Súbahdár assented, and, returning to his army, set out and arrived at the capital the same evening. Clive, having sent friendly letters to the other chief conspirators, made a short march of six miles to the village of Baptá, and encamped there for the evening. At noon the day following he proceeded to Madhupur, whence he despatched Messrs. Watts and Walsh, with an escort of 100 sipáhís, to arrange for the payments noted in a preceding page. These soon found that the treasury was not at the moment equal to the demand. They arranged accordingly that one moiety should be paid down: of this moiety two-thirds in hard coin, one-third in jewels and plate; that the second moiety should be discharged by three equal payments, extending over three years.

Whilst these negotiations were progressing, Clive, having ascertained that the other chief conspirators had accepted the terms offered to them, entered the city of Murshidábád (July 29), attended by 200 Europeans and 300 sipáhís, and took up his quarters in the palace of Murádbágh, his followers encamping in the garden attached to it. Here he was waited upon by Míran, the eldest son of Mír Jafar, and with him, he proceeded to the Súbahdár's palace, where Mír Jafar and his principal officers were waiting to receive him. Clive, after saluting Mír Jafar, led him to the _masnad_, and, despite some affected unwillingness on the part of the Mír, seated him upon it, hailed him with the usual {112}forms as Súbahdár, offering at the same time a Nazar of 100 _ashrafís_.[8] He then, through an interpreter, addressed the assembled nobles, congratulated them on the change of masters, and urged them to be faithful to Mír Jafar. The usual ceremonies followed, and the new ruler was publicly proclaimed throughout the city.

[Footnote 8: The value of an _ashrafía_, at a later period called by the English 'Gold Muhr,' was about 1_l_. 11_s_. 8_d_. A 'Nazar' is a gift offered and received when people of rank pay their respects to a prince. It is more properly called 'Nazráná.']

It is impossible to quit this subject without recording, as briefly as possible, the fate of the relative Mír Jafar had betrayed and supplanted. Siráj-up-daulá, fleeing, as we have seen, from the field of Plassey, had reached Murshidábád the same night. The next morning the news of the total rout of his army reached him. He remained in his palace till dusk, then, accompanied by his favorite wife, he embarked on a boat, hoping to find refuge in the camp of M. Law, who was advancing from Bhágalpur. But at Rájmahál the strength of the rowers gave out, and the young prince rested for the night in the buildings of a deserted garden. There he was discovered, and, taken back, was made over to Mír Jafar. The interview which followed will recall to the English historical student the scene between James II and the Duke of Monmouth. There was the same vain imploring for life on the one side, the same inexorable refusal on the other. That same night Siráj-up-daulá was stabbed to death in his cell.

{113}Another scene, scarcely less revolting in its details, had occurred the preceding day. I have mentioned the two treaties made by the conspirators, the one the real treaty, the other a counterpart, drawn up to deceive Aminchand. In the distribution of the plunder, it had become necessary to disclose the truth to the wily Bengal speculator. For him, there need be but little pity. Entrusted with the secrets of the conspirators, he had threatened to betray them unless twenty lakhs of rupees should be secured to him in the general agreement. He was, in a word--to use an expression much in use at the present day--a 'blackmailer.' Clive and the officers with whom he was acting thought it justifiable to deceive such a man. The hour of his awakening had now arrived. The two treaties were produced, and Aminchand was somewhat brutally informed by Mr. Scrafton that the treaty in which his name appeared was a sham; that he was to have nothing. The sudden shock is said to have alienated his reason. But if so, the alienation was only temporary. He proceeded on a pilgrimage to Malda, and for a time abstained from the business. But the old records of Calcutta show that he soon returned to his trade, for his name appears in many of the transactions in which the English were interested after the departure of Clive.

Nor was the dealing with Aminchand the only matter connected with the distribution of the spoil which caused ill-feeling. There had been much bitterness stirred up in the army by the fact that the {114}sailors who had fought at Plassey should receive their share of the amount promised to the navy in addition to that which would accrue to them as fighting men. A mixed Committee, composed of representatives of each branch of the military service, had decided against the claims of the sailors to draw from both sources, and Clive appealed to confirm it. But Clive, who, in matters of discipline, was unbending, overruled the decision of the Committee, placed its leader, Captain Armstrong, under arrest, and dissolved the Committee. In a dignified letter, Clive pointed out to the Committee their error and drew from them an apology. But the feeling rankled. It displayed itself a little later in the acquittal of

Captain Armstrong by a court-martial. In other respects, the distribution of the money was harmful, for it led to excesses among officers and men, and, consequently, to a large increase in mortality.

Meanwhile, the new Súbahdár began to find that the State-cushion was not altogether a bed of roses. The enormous sums demanded by his English allies, and by other adherents, had forced him, as soon as Clive had left for Calcutta, to apply the screw to the wealthier of his new subjects. Even his fellow conspirators felt the burden. Rájá Duláb Rám, whom he had made Finance Minister, with the right to appropriate to himself five percent. on all payments made by the Treasury, retired in dudgeon to his palace, summoned his friends, and refused all intercourse with Mír Jafar. The Rájá of Purniah and the Governor of {115}Bihár went into rebellion. The disaffection reached even the distant city of Dháká, where the son of Sarfaráz, the representative of the ancient family ruling in Bengal, lived in retirement and hope. Under these circumstances Mír Jafar, though he well knew what it would cost him, made an application for assistance to Clive.

The English leader had expected the application. He had recognized long before that, in the East, power depends mainly on the length of the purse, and that, from having exhausted his treasury, Mír Jafar would be forced to sue to h_in form pauperis_. Clive had studied the situation in all its aspects. The blow he had given to native rule by the striking down of the late Súbahdár had rendered absolute government, such as that exercised by Siráj-up-upulá, impossible. Thenceforth it had become indispensable that the English should supervise the native rule, leaving to the Súbahdár the initiative and the semblance. Clive had reason to believe that whilst Mír Jafar would be unwilling to play such a rôle, he would yet, under pressure, play it. He had seen that the new ruler was so enamored of the paraphernalia of power that, rather than renounce it, he would agree to whatever terms he might impose which would secure for him nominal authority. There was but one point regarding which he had doubts, and that was whether the proud Muhammadan nobles to whom, in the days of the glories of the Mughal empire, great estates had been granted in Bengal, would tamely submit to a system {116}which would give to the Western invaders all the actual power, and to the chief of their class and religion only the outer show.

The application form Mír Jafar, then, found Clive in the mood to test this question. Mír Jafar had thrown himself into his hands; he would use the chance to make it clear that he intended to be the real master, whilst prepared to render to the Súbahdár the respect and homage due to his position. Accordingly, he started at once (November 17) for Murshidábád with all his available troops, now reduced at Calcutta to 400 English and 1300 sipáhís, and reached that place on the 25th, bringing with him the disaffected Rájá of Purina. His peace he made with the Mír Jafar; then, joined by the 250 Europeans he had left at Kásimbázár, he proceeded to Rájmahál and encamped there close to the army of the Súbahdár, who had marched it thither with the object of coercing Bihár.

This was Clive's opportunity. Bihár was very restive, and the Súbahdár could not coerce its nobles without the aid of the English. Clive declined to render that aid unless the Súbahdár should, before one of his soldiers marched, pay up all the arrears due to the English, and should execute every article of the treaty he had recently signed. For Mír Jafar the dilemma was terrible. He had not the money;

he had made enemies by his endeavors to raise it. In this trouble, he bethought him of Rájá Duláb Rám, recently his Finance Minister, but whom {117}he had subsequently alienated. Through Clive's mediation, a reconciliation was patched up with the Rájá. Then the matter was arranged in the manner Clive had intended it should be, by giving the English a further hold on the territories of the Súbahdár.

It was agreed that Clive should receive orders on the treasury of Murshidábád for twelve and a half lakhs of rupees; assignments on the revenues of Bardwán, Kishangarh, and Húglí for ten and a half: for the payments becoming due in the following April, assignments on the same districts for nineteen lakhs: then the cession of the lands south of Calcutta, so long deferred, was made--the annual rental being the sum of 222,958 rupees. These arrangements having been completed, Clive accompanied the Súbahdár to the capital of Bihár, the famous city of Patná. There they both remained, the Súbahdár awaiting the receipt of the imperial patents confirming him in his office; Clive resolved, whatever were the personal inconvenience to himself, not to quit Patná so long as the Súbahdár should remain there. They stayed there three months, a period which Clive utilized to the best advantage, as it seemed to him at the moment, of his countrymen. The province of Bihár was the seat of the saltpeter manufacturer. It was a monopoly[9] farmed to agents, who re-sold the saltpeter on terms bringing very large profits. Clive proposed to the {118}Súbahdár that the East India Company should become the farmers, and offered a higher sum than any at which the monopoly had been previously rated. Mír Jafar was too shrewd a man not to recognize the enormous advantages which must accrue to his foreign protectors by his acquiescence in a scheme that would place in their hands the most important trade in the country. But he felt the impossibility of resistance. He was a bird in the hands of the fowler, and he agreed.

[Footnote 9: The possession of this monopoly became the cause of the troubles that followed the departure of Clive, and led to the life-and-death struggle with Mír Kásim.]

At length (April 14) the looked-for patents arrived. Accompanying that which gave to the usurpation of Mír Jafar the imperial sanction was a patent for Clive, creating him a noble of the Mughal empire, with the rank and title of a Mansabdar[10] of 6000 horses. The investiture took place the day following. Then, after marching to Bárh, the two armies separated, the Súbahdár proceeding to Murshidábád; Clive, after a short stay at that place, to Calcutta.

[Footnote 10: For the nature of Mansab, and the functions of the holder of a Mansab (or Mansabdar) the reader is referred to Blochmann's _Ain-í-Akbarí_. By the original regulations of Akbar, who founded the order, the Mansabdars ranked from the Dahbashi, often Commander-in-Chief, to the Doh Hazári, Commander of 10,000 horses, to the Mansabdars of 6000 downwards. Vide _Ain-í-Akbarí_ (Blochmann's), p. 237 and onwards.]

Clive had returned to Calcutta, on May 24, absolute master of the situation. He had probed to the bottom the character of the Súbahdár and had realized that so long as he should remain in India, and Mír Jafar on the _masnad_, the English need fear no attack. But, in the East, one man's life, especially the {119}life of a usurper, is never secure. In those days the risks he incurred were infinitely greater than they are now. Clive had noted the ill-disguised impatience of several of the powerful nobles, more especially that of

Míran, the son, and Mír Kásim, the son-in-law, of the Súbahdár. He had left, then, the greater part of his English soldiers at Kásimbázár, close to the native capital, to watch events, whilst he returned to Calcutta to trace there the plan of a fortress which would secure the English against attack. The fort so traced, received the name of its predecessor, built by Job Charnock in the reign of King William III, and called after him, Fort William.

Nearly one month later, June 20, there arrived from England despatches, penned after learning the recapture of Calcutta, but before any knowledge of the events which had followed that recapture, ordering a new constitution for the administering of the Company's possessions in Bengal. The text of the constitution, ridiculous under any circumstances, was utterly unadapted to the turn events had taken. It nominated ten men, not one of whom was competent for the task, to administer the affairs of Bengal. The name Clive was not included among the ten names. It was not even mentioned. Fortunately for the Company, the ten men nominated had a clearer idea of their fitness than had their honorable masters. With one consent, they represented the true situation to the Court of Directors, and then, with the same unanimity, requested Clive {120}to accept the office of President, and to exercise its functions, until the pleasure of the Court should be known. Clive could not but accede to their request.

For, indeed, it was no time for weak administration and divided counsels. Again the French attempted to recover the position in Southern India that Clive had wrested from them. Count Lally, one of the brilliant victors of Fontenoy, had been sent to Pondicherry with considerable force, and the news had just arrived that he was marching on Tanjore, having recalled Bussy and his troops from the court of the

Súbahdár of the Deccan. With the news, there had come also a request that the Government of Bengal would return to the sister Presidency the troops lent to her by the latter in the hour of the former's need to recover Calcutta.

Clive felt all the urgency of the request; the possible danger of refusing to comply with it; the full gravity of the situation at Madras. He also was one of those who had been lent. If the troops were to return, it was he who should lead them back. But he felt strongly that his place, and their place also, was in Bengal. Especially was it so in the presence of the rumors, already circulating, of great successes achieved by Lally, and by the French fleet. Such rumors, followed by his departure, would certainly incite the nobles of Bengal and Bihár, with or without Mír Jafar, to strike for the independence which they felt, one and all, he had wrested from them.

Matters, indeed, in the provinces of Bengal and {121}Bihár had come to bear a very threatening aspect. The treasury of Mír Jafar was exhausted by his payments; his nobles were disaffected; the moneyed classes were bitterly hostile. Threatened on his northern frontier by a rebellious son of the King of Delhi and by the Nawáb-Wazír of Oudh, Mír Jafar was in the state of mind which compels men of his stamp to have recourse to desperate remedies. For a moment he thought seriously of calling the Maráthás to his assistance. Then the conviction forced itself upon him that the remedy would be worse than the disease, and he renounced the idea. At last, when the army of the rebel prince had penetrated within Bihár and was approaching Patná, he resigned himself to the inevitable and besought abjectly the assistance of Clive.

Clive had resolved to help him when affairs in Southern India reached a point that required his immediate attention.

A letter from the Rájá of Vizianagram reached him, informing him that the effect of the recall by Lally from Aurangábád of the troops under Bussy had been to leave the Northern Sirkárs[11] without sufficient protection; that he and other Rájás had risen in revolt, and urgently demanded the despatch thither of some English troops, by whose aid they could expel the few Frenchmen left there. It was characteristic of Clive to seize the points of a difficult situation. Few men who had to meet on their front a dangerous invasion would have dared to despatch, to a distant point, the troops he {122}had raised to repel that invasion, remaining himself to meet it from resources he would improvise. But, without a moment's hesitation or a solitary misgiving, Clive recognized that the opportunity had come to him to complete the work he had begun, six years before, in Southern India; that a chance presented itself to transfer the great influence exercised by Bussy at the court of the Súbahdár of the Deccan to his nation. Leaving to himself then the care of Bengal and Bihár he directed a trusted officer, Colonel Forde, to proceed (October 12) with 500 Europeans, 2000 sipáhís, and some guns to Vizagapatam, to unite there with the Rájá's troops, to take command; and to expel the French from the Northern Sirkárs: then, if it were possible, to assume at the court of the Súbahdár the influence which the French had till then exercised. It is only necessary here to say that Forde, who was one of the great Indian soldiers of the century, carried both points with skill and discretion. He beat the French in detail, and compelled them to yield their fortresses; and, when the Súbahdár marched to their aid, he succeeded, with rare tact, in inducing him to cede to the English the whole of the territories he had conquered, and to transfer the paramount influence at his court to the English. The victories of Forde laid the foundation of a predominance which, placed some forty years later on a definite basis by the great Marquess Wellesley, exists to the present day. It is not too much to assert that this splendid result was due to {123}the unerring sagacity, the daring under difficult circumstances, of Robert Clive.

[Footnote 11: The districts of Ganjám, Vizagapatam, Godávari, and Krishna.]

Meanwhile, the solicitations of Mír Jafar increased in importunity. Even the Great Mughal called upon Clive, as a Mansabdar, to assist him to repress the rebellion of his son. Clive did not refuse. As soon as his preparation had been completed, he set out, February 1759, for Murshidábád with 450 Europeans and 2500 sipáhís, leaving the care of Calcutta to a few sick and invalids. He reached Murshidábád on the 8th of March, and, accompanied by the Mír Jafar's army, entered Patná on the 8th of April. But the rumor of his march had been sufficient. Four days before the date mentioned the rebellious prince evacuated his positions before the city, and, eventually, sought refuge in Bundelkhand. Clive entered Patná in triumph; put down with a strong hand the disturbances in its vicinity; and then returned to Calcutta, in time enough to hear of the victorious course of Forde, although not of its more solid result.

Before he had quitted Patná, Mír Jafar had conferred upon him, as a personal jágír,[12] the Zamíndárí {124}of the entire districts south of Calcutta then rented by the East India Company.

[Footnote 12: A jágír is land given by a government as a reward for services rendered. A Zamíndárí, under the Mughal government, meant a tract, or tracts of land held immediately by the government on the condition of paying the rent it. By the deed given to Clive, the East India Company, which had agreed to pay the rents of those lands to the Súbahdár, would pay them to Clive to whom the Súbahdár had, by this deed, transferred his rights. It may here be added that the Company denied the right of Clive to the rents which amounted to 30,000 pounds per annum, and great bitterness ensued. The matter was ultimately compromised.]

Clive had scarcely returned to Calcutta when there ensued complications with the Dutch.

During the sixteenth and seventeenth centuries, Holland had posed in the East as a rival, often a successful rival, of the three nations which had attempted to found settlements in those regions. She had established a monopoly of trade with the Moluccas, had possessed herself of several islands in the vicinity of the Straits, had expelled Portugal from Malacca (1641), Ceylon (1658), the Celebes (1663), and the most important of her conquests on the coasts of Southern India (1665). At the beginning of the eighteenth century, the Dutch-Indian Company possessed the east seven administrations; four directorial posts; four military commands; and four factories. The Company was rich and had but few debts.

Amongst the minor settlements, it had made was the town of Chinsurah, on the Húglí, twenty miles above Calcutta. Chinsurah was a subordinate station, but, until the contests between the Nawáb and the English, it had been a profitable possession. We have seen how, under the pressure of Clive, Mír Jafar had made to the English some important trade concessions. It was certain that sooner or later, these would affect the trade, the profits, and the self-respect, of the European rivals of Great Britain. Prominent traders amongst these were the Dutch. Amongst {125}the changes which they felt most bitterly were (1) the monopoly, granted to the English, of the saltpeter trade; (2) the right to search all vessels coming up the Húglí; (3) the employment of no other than English pilots. These injuries, as they considered them, rankled in their breasts, and they resolved to put a stop to them. To effect that purpose they entered into secret negotiations with Mír Jafar. These, after a time, ended in the entering into an agreement in virtue of which, whilst the Dutch covenanted to despatch to the Húglí a fleet and army sufficiently strong to expel the English from Bengal, the Súbahdár pledged himself to prepare with the greatest secrecy an army to co-operate with them. This agreement was signed in November 1758, just after Clive had despatched Forde, with all the troops then available, to the Northern Sirkárs, but before his march to Patná, recorded, with its consequences, in the preceding pages. The secret had been well kept, for Clive had no suspicion of the plot. He knew he had the Súbahdár in the hollow of his hand, so far as related to the princes of the soil; he knew the French were powerless to aid the Súbahdár: and he never thought of the little settlement of Chinsurah.

In June 1759, just following the return of Clive to Calcutta, the Mír Jafar received from the Dutch a secret intimation that their plans were approaching maturity. He stayed then but a short time at the English seat of government, but returned {126}thither in October, to be at hand when the expected crisis should occur. Meanwhile, rumors had got about that a considerable Dutch fleet was approaching the Húglí, and, in fact, a large Dutch vessel, with Malayan soldiers, did arrive at Diamond Harbour. Clive had at once demanded from the Dutch authorities an explanation, at the same time that he innocently apprised

Mír Jafar of the circumstance and the rumor. The Dutch authorities explained that the ship had been bound for Nágapatnam, but had been forced by the stress of weather to seek refuge in the Húglí.

In October, whilst Mír Jafar was actually in Calcutta, the Dutch made their spring. It was a very serious attack, for the Dutch had four ships, carrying every thirty-six guns; two, each carrying twenty-six; one, carrying sixteen, and had on board these 700 European soldiers and 800 Malays: at Chinsurah they had 150 Europeans, and a fair number of native levies: behind them, they had the Súbahdár. To meet them Clive had but three Indiamen, each carrying thirty guns, and a small despatch-boat. Of soldiers, he had, actually in Calcutta and the vicinity, 330 Europeans, and 1200 sipáhís. The nearest of the detachments in the country was too distant to reach the scene of action in time to take part in the impending struggle. There was aid, however, approaching, that he knew not of.

Clive is revealed in danger. In its presence, his splendid qualities shone forth with a brilliancy which {127}has never been surpassed. His was the soul that animated the material figures around him. His the daring with which he could inspire his subordinates; imbue them with his high courage; and make them, likewise, 'conquer the impossible.'

His conduct on the occasion I am describing is pre-eminently worthy of study. A short interview with Mír Jafar filled his mind with grave suspicions. He did not show them. He even permitted Mír Jafar to proceed to Húglí to have an interview with the Dutch authorities. But when the Súbahdár despatched to him from that place a letter in which he stated that he had simply granted to the Dutch some indulgences concerning their trade, he drew the correct conclusion and prepared to meet the double danger.

In his summary of the several courses, he would have to adopt the dismissed altogether the Súbahdár from his mind. Him he feared not. With the Dutch, he would deal and deal summarily. He had already despatched special messengers to summon every available man from the outposts. He now called out the militia, 300 men, five-sixths of whom were Europeans, to defend the town and fort; he formed half a troop of volunteer horsemen, and enlisted as volunteer infantry all the men who could not ride; he ordered the despatch-boat to sail with all speed to the Arakan coast, where she would find a squadron under Admiral Cornish ready to send him aid; he ordered up, to lie just below the fort, the three Indiamen of {128}which I have spoken: he strengthened the two batteries commanding the most important passages of the river near Calcutta, and mounted guns on the nascent Fort William. Then, when he had completed all that 'Prudentia' could suggest, the rival goddess, 'Fortuna'[13] smiled upon him. Just as he was completing his preparations, Colonel Forde and Captain Knox, fresh from the conquest of the Northern Sirkárs, arrived to strengthen his hand. To the former Clive assigned the command of the whole of his available force in the field: to the latter, the charge of the two batteries.

[Footnote 13: 'Nullum numen best si sit Prudentia; nos te, Nos facimus Fortuna, deam.' _Juvenal_.]

Up to that period the Dutch had endeavored to pose as peaceful traders. But no sooner had their negotiations with Mír Jafar been completed, and they had received his permission to ascend to Chinsurah, than they threw off the mask, and sent an ultimatum to Clive threatening vengeance unless the English should renounce their claim of the right of search, and redress the other grievances they enumerated. Clive replied that in all his actions he had been guided by the authority vested in him by the Súbahdár, the representative of the Great Mughal; that he was powerless in the matter; but that if they would refer their complaints to the Súbahdár, he would gladly act the part of mediator. The Dutch commander, however, paid no heed to this somewhat vague reply but acted as though it were a {129}declaration of war. For, on receipt of Clive's letter he attacked and captured seven small vessels lying off Falta, among them the despatch-boat above referred to, tore down the English colors, and transferred the guns and material to their ships. Then, having plundered the few houses on the riverbanks, he continued his upward course, with his ships, although, from the want of pilots, their progress was necessarily slow.

Clive, on hearing of these demonstrations, prepared to act on the instant. First, he sent a despatch to the Súbahdár, telling him that the quarrel between the two European nations must be fought out alone, adding, however, to test Mír Jafar, a paragraph to the effect that the Súbahdár would convince him of his sincerity and attachment if he would directly surround their (the Dutch) subordinates, and distress them in 'the country to the utmost.' Then he ordered Forde to occupy Bárnagar on the left bank of the Húglí, five miles from Calcutta; to cross thence with his troops and four field pieces to Shirirámpur, nine miles distant; to be ready, either there or beyond it, to intercept the Dutch troops, in the event of their trying to reach Chinsurah by land. Then, learning that the Dutch ships had progressed as far as the Sankrál reach, just below the fire of the English batteries, and were landing their troops with directions to march directly on Chinsurah, he issued orders for immediate action.

Recognizing on the instant that, by landing, the {130}enemy's troops had severed themselves from their base--the ships--he despatched Knox to join Forde and sent information to the latter of the probable route the enemy's troops would take, leaving it to him to deal with them as he might consider advisable. Then he sent orders to Commodore Wilson, the senior of the captains of the Indiamen, to demand from the Commander of the Dutch squadron a full apology for the insults he and his subordinates had been guilty of, the return of the individuals and of the plunder he and they had taken, and their immediate departure from the Húglí. Failing prompt compliance with all these demands, Wilson was to attack the enemy's squadron.

The scene that followed deserves to rank with the most glorious achievements of English sailors. The three captains were all built in the heroic mold. Not one of them felt a doubt of victory when they were ordered to attack a squadron in all respects more than double in numbers and weight of metal to their own. It must suffice here to say[14] that, the proposal of the English Commodore having been refused by the Dutch, the English captains bore down upon the enemy; after a contest of little more than two hours, captured or sank six of their ships; the seventh, hurrying out to sea, fell into the hands of two ships of war, then entering the river. Well {131}might the victors exclaim, in the language of our great national poet:--

'O, such a day,
So fought, so followed, and so fairly won,
Came not till now to dignify the times,
Since Caesar's fortunes.'

[Footnote 14: For a detailed account of this action see the author's _Decisive Battles of India_.]

This success left the Dutch soldiers, then on their way to Chinsurah, absolutely without a base. They could only find safety in success, and success was denied them. They were first repulsed by Forde in an attack they made on a position he had taken at Chandranagar, and the next day almost destroyed by the same gallant officer, joined by Knox, in a battle at the village of Biderra, nearly midway between Chandranagar and Chinsurah. Few victories have been more decisive. Of the 700 Europeans and 800 Malays who landed from the ships, 120 of the former and 200 of the latter were left dead on the field; 300, in about equal proportions, were wounded; and the remainder, except 60 Dutch and 250 Malays, were taken, prisoners. Forde had under his command on this eventful day (November 25) 320 Europeans, 800 sipáhís, and 50 European volunteer cavalry. The previous day, reckoning that he would have to fight the enemy with his inferior numbers, he had sent a note to Clive asking for implicit instructions. Clive, who was playing whist when the note reached him, knowing with whom he was dealing, wrote across it, in pencil: 'Dear Forde, Fight them immediately: I will send you the order {132}in Council tomorrow,' and sent back the messenger with it.

The two victories were in all respects decisive. Never again did the Dutch trouble the tranquillity of India. Mír Jafar was cowed. Three days after the victory of Biderra, his son, Míran, arrived from Murshidábád with 6,000 horses, for the purpose, he explained, of exterminating the Dutch. Clive, always merciful in victory, given to these, against their baffled confederate, the protection which he considered due to a foe no longer to be dreaded.

Clive now regarded the British position in Bengal so secure that he might return to England to enjoy there the repose and the position he had acquired. He had compressed into three years achievements the most momentous, the most marvelous, the most enduring, recorded in the history of his country. Landing with a small force below Calcutta in the last days of 1756, he had compelled the Súbahdár, who had been responsible for the Black Hole tragedy, though guiltless of designing it,[15] to evacuate Calcutta, to witness without interfering his capture of Chandranagar. Determined, then, in the interests of his country, to place matters in Bengal on such a footing that a repetition of the tragedy of 1756 should be impossible, he resolved to replace Siráj-up-daulá, himself the son of a usurper, with a native chieftain {133}who should owe everything to the English, and who would probably allow himself to be guided by them in his policy. To this end, he formed a conspiracy among his nobles, fomented discontent among his people, and finally forced him to appeal to arms. At Plassey Clive risked everything on the fidelity to himself of the conspirators with whom he had allied himself. They were faithful. He gained the battle, not gloriously but decisively, and became from the morrow of the victory the lord paramount of the noble whom he placed then on the _masnad_. Possibly it was partly policy that impelled him to give his nominee no chance from the beginning. Certain it is, that Mír Jafar was, from the moment of his accession, so handicapped by the compulsion to make to his allies enormous payments, that his life, from that moment to the hour of his deposition, presently to be related, was not worth living. The commercial concessions which Clive had forced from him gave the English an _imperium in imperio_. But the Súbahdár was in the toils. When the invasion came from the north he tried his utmost to avoid asking for the aid of

Clive. But Clive, who had sent his best soldiers to conquer the Northern Sirkárs, and to establish permanent relations with the Súbahdár of the Deccan--relations which secured to England a permanent predominance in the most important districts of southern India--was indispensable. His assistance, given in a manner which could not fail to impress the natives of India--for the enemy fled at his approach--riveted the {134}chains on the Súbahdár. Then came the invasion of the Dutch. For the first time, a superior hostile force of Europeans landed on the shores of British India. The Súbahdár, anxious above all things to recover his freedom of action, promised them his assistance. Clive shone out here, more magnificently than he had shone before, as the undaunted hero. Disdaining to notice the action of the Súbahdár, he gave all his attention to the European invaders; with far inferior means he baffled their schemes; and crushed them in a manner such as would make them and did make them, remember and repent the audacity which had allowed them to imagine that they could impose their will on the victor of Káveripák and Plassey. He had made the provinces he had conquered secure, if only the rule which was to follow his own should be based on justice, against the native rulers; secure forever against European rivals assailing it from the sea.

Clive now regarded the British position in Bengal so secure that he might return to England to enjoy there the repose and the position he had acquired. He had compressed into three years achievements the most momentous, the most marvelous, the most enduring, recorded in the history of his country. Landing with a small force below Calcutta in the last days of 1756, he had compelled the Súbahdár, who had been responsible for the Black Hole tragedy, though guiltless of designing it,[15] to evacuate Calcutta, to witness without interfering his capture of Chandranagar. Determined, then, in the interests of his country, to place matters in Bengal on such a footing that a repetition of the tragedy of 1756 should be impossible, he resolved to replace Siráj-up-daulá, himself the son of a usurper, with a native chieftain {133}who should owe everything to the English, and who would probably allow himself to be guided by them in his policy. To this end, he formed a conspiracy among his nobles, fomented discontent among his people, and finally forced him to appeal to arms. At Plassey Clive risked everything on the fidelity to himself of the conspirators with whom he had allied himself. They were faithful. He gained the battle, not gloriously but decisively, and became from the morrow of the victory the lord paramount of the noble whom he placed then on the _masnad_. Possibly it was partly policy that impelled him to give his nominee no chance from the beginning. Certain it is, that Mír Jafar was, from the moment of his accession, so handicapped by the compulsion to make to his allies enormous payments, that his life, from that moment to the hour of his deposition, presently to be related, was not worth living. The commercial concessions which Clive had forced from him gave the English an _imperium in imperio_. But the Súbahdár was in the toils. When the invasion came from the north he tried his utmost to avoid asking for the aid of Clive. But Clive, who had sent his best soldiers to conquer the Northern Sirkárs, and to establish permanent relations with the Súbahdár of the Deccan--relations which secured to England a permanent predominance in the most important districts of southern India--was indispensable. His assistance, given in a manner which could not fail to impress the natives of India--for the enemy fled at his approach--riveted the {134}chains on the Súbahdár. Then came the invasion of the Dutch. For the first time, a superior hostile force of Europeans landed on the shores of British India. The Súbahdár, anxious above all things to recover his freedom of action, promised them his assistance. Clive shone out here, more magnificently than he had shone before, as the undaunted hero. Disdaining to notice the action of the Súbahdár, he gave all his attention to the European invaders; with far inferior means he baffled their schemes; and crushed them in a manner such as would make them and did make them, remember and repent the audacity which had allowed them to imagine that they could impose their will on the victor of Káveripák and Plassey. He had made the provinces he had conquered secure, if only the rule which was to follow his own should be based on justice, against the native rulers; secure forever against European rivals assailing it from the sea.

[Footnote 15: Siráj-up-daulá had given instructions that the prisoners should be safely cared for, and had then gone to sleep. It was the brutality of his subordinate officers which caused the catastrophe.]

That, during this period, he had committed faults, is only to say that he was human. But, unfortunately, some of his faults were so grave as to cast a lasting stain on a career in many respects worthy of the highest admiration. The forging of the name of Admiral Watson, although the name was attached to the deed with, it is believed, his approval,[16] was a crime light in comparison with the purpose for which it {135}was done--the deceiving of the Bengálí, Aminchand. Aminchand was indeed a scoundrel, a blackmailer, a man who had said: 'Pay me well, or I will betray your secrets.' But that was no reason why Clive should fight him with his weapons: should descend to the arena of deceit in which the countrymen of Aminchand were past masters. Possibly the atmosphere he breathed in such society was answerable, to a great extent, for this deviation from the path of honor. But the stain remains. No washing will remove it. It affected him whilst he still lived, and will never disappear.

[Footnote 16: In his evidence before the Committee of the House of Commons Clive said regarding the fictitious treaty: 'It was sent to Admiral Watson, who objected to the signing of it; but, to the best of his remembrance, gave the gentleman who carried it (Mr. Lushington) leave to sign his name upon it.']

Then again, as to his dealings with Siráj-up-daulá and Mír Jafar. The whole proceedings of Clive after his capture of Calcutta prove that he intended to direct all his policy to the removal of that young prince from the _masnad_. Some have thought that the Black Hole tragedy was the cause of this resolve. But this can hardly be so, for Mír Jafar, the commander-in-chief of the army which seized Calcutta in 1756, was equally implicated in that transaction. The suggestion that Siráj-up-daulá was intriguing with the French at Haidarábád is equally untenable, for Clive knew he had little cause to fear their hostility. Clive not only expelled that prince but, by his policy, his extortions, and his insistence to obtain control of the saltpeter traffic, rendered it impossible for his successor to govern. Success attended his policy so long as he remained on the spot to control his subordinates, but it was inevitable that, sooner or later, there would come {136}a revulsion. The warlike natives of Bihár had not been conquered, and they knew it. They had helped Clive, not that they should become subject to the foreigner from the sea, but that they might have a native ruler whom they trusted, in place of one whom they disliked. When they realized that the result of this change was not only subjection to the islanders but impoverishment to themselves, they broke into what was called rebellion and showed on many a bloody field that it was not they, only Siráj-up-daulá, who had been conquered at Plassey.

This was the most dangerous legacy of policy and action of Clive. He recognized its shadowy existence. He wrote to his successor, Mr. Vansittart, when he transferred to him his own office, that the only danger he had to dread in Bengal was that which might arise from venality and corruption. He might have added that the spoils of Plassey had created a state of society in which those vices were prominent; that the saltpeter monopoly, with the duties and exemptions which had followed its acquisition, had confirmed them. The Súbahdár himself recognized the new danger which would follow the departure of Clive. In his mind, he was the moderator who, satisfied himself, would have stayed in the hands of others. To quiet the newcomers there would be fresh rapacity and more stringent despoiling. He felt, to use the expression of the period when Clive quitted Bengal, that 'the soul was departing from the body.'

Before the entrance of Mr. Vansittart, Clive gave Mr. Holwell of Black 137-Hole infamy a charge on February 15, 1760. He had proposed Major Calliaud as Commander of the Forces with the Court's approval. He retired around the same time as four other members of his council.

Siráj-ud-forces daulá's are under the command of MR JAFAR. joined Clive at age 79 86: fought with Siráj-up-doula, 88: reconciliation, 88: oath of fealty and pledge to oppose Clive, 88 and 91: his conversations with Mr. Watts 92: denied that Watts was a spy. 92: threatening to exterminate the English positive despatch from, the position of his soldiers at Plassey, and 92 Interview 97 with Siráj-up-doula 100: the lingering of his soldiers, 103: asked Clive for an interview, 105: taken to the camp to receive the designation Súbahdár, 107: His agreements and terms with Clive, 107-8: a wealthy family in Bihár, 109: Al Vardi Khán's officer; 109: spouse of Al Vardi Khán's sister; 109: The military Baksh, 109: went to Calcutta 109: the meeting he had with Clive, 110: traveled to Murshidabad, Clive was received by the number 111.

following his encounter with Clive, 110, he traveled to Murshidabad, 111, where he saw Clive, 111, and declared Sbahdár, 112: requested aid from Clive, 115, 121: His army at Rájmál 116: try to intimidate Bihár 116: at Patná, where I met Clive. 117: marched to Bárh with Clive, 118: arrived back in Murshidabad, 118: Exhausted treasury, 121: awarded Clive the jágr of the Zamndár, obliged to resign, 153 required to live under English protection, and 123 Mr. Kásim displaces 153, the English reinstate 153, 158 and 159: his passing 159, 160: left money in Clive's will. 178: Lord Clive's Fund was established.

MR KSIM, Mr . Jafar's son-in-law, 119, 152: Mr . Jafar's envoy, 152: aspired to succeed MMoran 152: his bribing was effective, 152: Mr . Jafar was to be replaced by, 152: made their way to Patna, 153: Sbahdár established, 153:

good ruler, 153: fort moved to Munger 153: army restructured, 154: transit tasks eliminated, 155: war preparations, 155: Markar, leading his army, left for Patná. Samru was despatched to Baksar to drive the English away in Chapter 155. In Chapter 156, the English were intercepted and soundly defeated. defeated in 156 at Kátwá, 156 at Gheriá, 156: sought sanctuary at Oudh after Patna fell. 157: defeated at Baksar; 158: passed away in Delhi.

General Siráj-ud-daula, Mádan, was killed at Plassey in 100.

The commander of Mr. Jafar's forces, M.R. MMehdiKhan, 155, proceeded to MMungerto to report to Mr. Jafar.

Capt.-Lieut. MMOLITORat Council of War, 93.

Famous Maratha soldier MORRI RO was sent to protect Trichinopoli at age 26, dispatched to aid Clive at Arcot at age 55, marched with Clive to Arni at age 56, beat the French at age 57 and 58, and helped Lawrence at age 68.

MORSE, Mr., Governor of Madras, 15, 33; he supported Clive; he rejected the French Governor's request that the two settlements maintain their neutrality; he begged in vain protection from Anwar-Uddin, and he was 35.

9 798887 838625

Printed by Libri Plureos GmbH in Hamburg,
Germany